STARTING ECOLOGY

Pond and Stream

Written and
photographed by

Colin S.Milkins

Artist: Roger Fereday

Wayland

STARTING ECOLOGY

Pond and Stream

Seashore

Wasteland

Wood

Editor: Sarah Doughty

First published in 1994 by
Wayland (Publishers) Ltd
61 Western Road, Hove,
East Sussex, BN3 1JD, England

British Library Cataloguing in Publication Data
Milkins, Colin S.
Pond and Stream. (Starting Ecology Series)
I. Title II. Series
574.5

ISBN 0 7502 0823 6

Typeset by Dorchester Typesetting Group Ltd, England
Printed and bound in Belgium by Casterman S.A.

What is ecology?

Ecology is the study of the way plants and animals live together in a habitat. A scientist who studies this is called an ecologist. An ecologist finds out about a habitat by observing the area and carrying out experiments. If you do the projects in this book, you will be an ecologist too.

Always investigate ponds and streams as a group with a parent or teacher, and never wander off on your own. Take great care near water.

CONTENTS

The words in **bold** are explained
in the glossary on page 30.

Ponds and streams

A pond is a large pool of still water. The water in a pond does not **flow** along as it does in a stream. A stream is always moving. It carries water to larger rivers which flow into the sea.

As a stream flows along, it mixes with air. When you watch a splashing stream, the white water is the stream mixing with air. This gives a stream more **oxygen** than pond water. Different types of animals live in ponds and streams. Some animals that live in streams would die if placed in a pond because there would not be enough oxygen in the water for them to breathe.

◄ *The water gushing in this stream is mixing with air.*

Animals have different shaped bodies to help them survive in ponds or streams. Some stream animals have flat bodies, which means that they can lie close to the stream **bed**, away from the fast **current**. Others, such as the mayfly **nymph** in the picture, are able to cling to weeds and stones which stops them being washed away. Many of the small animals that live in ponds could not cling tightly to stones in a stream and would be swept away.

▲ *A mayfly nymph can live in streams because it is able to hold on to rocks.*

To study ecology in ponds and streams, you will need to find a shallow pond and small stream in your area that you can study safely. It is best to go with friends or your school class. Always take an adult with you.

▶ *A small pond in a wood surrounded by waterside plants.*

Pond dipping

Find an area of open water to sweep up animals into the net.

Warning: Always go pond dipping with an adult, never by yourself.

It can be fun finding out what plants and animals live in ponds. Animals and plants find different places to live within a pond. Most of the tall plants, like sedges and rushes grow in the mud near the edges of the pond, which are sometimes called the margins. Some of the animals like to live in the margins where they can hide.

Plants also grow in the open water away from the margins, but they are floating and not rooted in the soil. Some animals prefer to live in the open water where they can find food. You can find out which animals like to live in the margins and which ones prefer the open water.

From the side of the pond make one sweep of the net in among the margin plants. Empty your catch into a large white tray filled with water. Then find an area of open water you can easily reach from the pond side. Make one sweep with your net in an area where there are not any weeds. It is important that you make only one sweep of the pond with your net for a fair test. Empty your catch into the tray.

▲ *With a sweep of the net you can pick up animals in the pond margins.*

Compare the number of animals in the two trays before putting them back in the pond. Do more animals live among the margin plants than in the open water?

▶ *The animals on the left of this picture were caught among the weeds. The ones on the right were swept up in open water.*

Catching shrimps

▲ *The freshwater shrimp is very active along the stream bed.*

The freshwater shrimp lives under stones in a stream. It is a small, very active creature that darts about the stream bed, looking for things to eat.

The bed of the stream is very uneven along its length. There are deeper parts where the water is calmer and moves more slowly. These parts of the stream are called flats, or pools. Between each flat the water is shallower, more disturbed and moves faster. These places are called riffles.

Find out if there are more shrimps in flats or riffles.

◄ *Kick the stones in front of the net so the water sweeps animals up into it.*

In a shallow area of the stream hold your net down on the bed of a flat. Kick the stones in front of the net five times. The flowing water will wash the shrimps into your net. Empty your catch into a white tray.

Now do the same in a riffle. Again, only kick the stones in front of the net five times. Compare your trays. Which has the most shrimps in it? When you have found out, return your shrimps to the stream.

Shrimps like to eat the remains of leaves that fall into the water from the trees above. Leaves are washed into the stream and gather in the flats at the bottom. Does the number of shrimps you found in flats and riffles tell you that this is where the shrimps are looking for food?

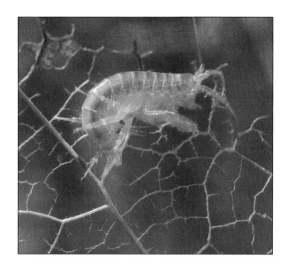

▲ *Nothing but the skeleton of this leaf is left after the shrimp has finished eating.*

▼ *Flats, or pools are the deeper parts of a stream. Riffles are shallow areas where the water moves faster.*

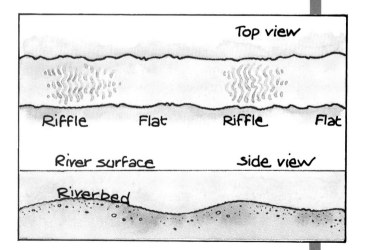

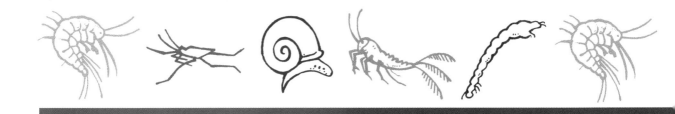

The backswimmer

▲ *The backswimmer uses its two hind legs as oars to swim quickly through the water.*

A common insect that lives in ponds is the greater water boatman. It is sometimes also called the backswimmer, because it swims upside-down on its back. It also rests under the water to take in the air which it stores around its body for use when it is under the water.

Catch a backswimmer from a pond and keep it in a jar of water. It swims very quickly, so is easiest to catch when it hangs still, upside-down in the water. Be careful how you handle the insect, as the backswimmer can give you a nasty bite.

◀ *Children studying the movements of a backswimmer they have caught.*

Find out what causes the backswimmer to swim the 'wrong way up'. When the insect swims in a pond, the light that falls on the pool comes from the sun above. Try an experiment to find out what your backswimmer does when the light comes from underneath.

Make a view-box like the one in the picture on the right. It is made out of a cardboard box, painted black on the inside, with a view-hole to look inside. A torch shines upwards on to the jar with your backswimmer in it.

Look through the spy hole at your backswimmer with the torch switched on. Is it now swimming the 'right way up'? Do you think that the way the light shines has told the backswimmer which way up to swim?

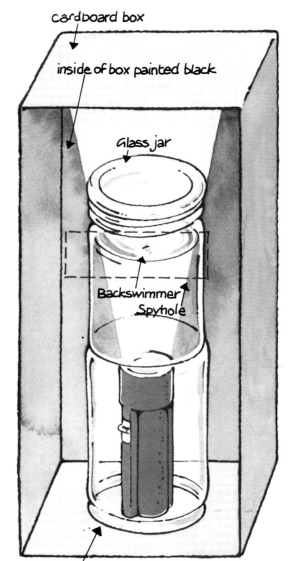

cardboard box

inside of box painted black

Glass jar

Backswimmer
Spyhole

Large glass jar big enough to take a small torch

Make a darkened box through which to watch your backswimmer.

Pond snails

▲ *The ramshorn snail takes in air from the water and from above the surface.*

▼ *Look carefully for the breathing hole of this great pond snail.*

Like all animals, pond snails need oxygen to breathe. They get some of their oxygen from the pond water. Pond snails such as the ramshorn and the great pond snail also breathe oxygen from the air above the water. Some ponds do not have a lot of oxygen in them, so snails living in these ponds have to come up to the top of the water to breathe more often.

You can investigate how often snails need to breathe. First, you will need to buy some pond snails from an aquarium shop. Make sure that the snails you buy are of a similar size. Keep your snails in a fish tank with some water and pond weed. The snails will live for a long time and even lay eggs.

Get an adult to help you boil some water. This will remove all the oxygen in the water. Leave the water until it is cold, and then pour it into a jar. Fill another jar with pond water that has not been boiled. This water will have a lot more oxygen in it.

Put five great pond snails into each jar. For both sets of snails, count the number of times all the snails come to the top of the water to breathe. Make a bar chart to show your results.

Did the snails in the boiled water come to the surface more often than the snails in the unboiled water?

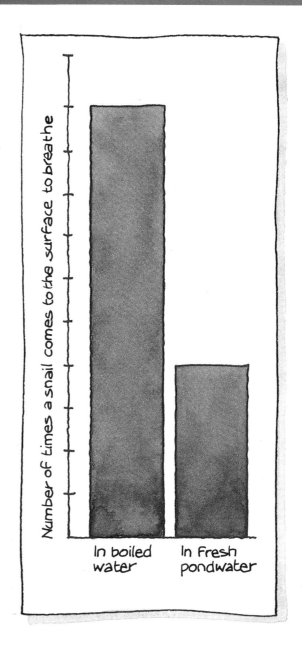

Bar charts showing how many times the snails moved to the surface of the water to breathe.

> **Warning:** Take care with very hot water. Get an adult to help you.

Water cleaners

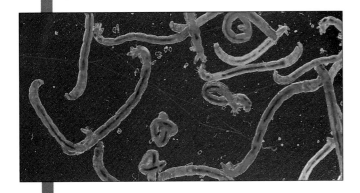

▲ *Bloodworms are small worm-like creatures, the larvae of the midge fly.*

▼ *The bloodworm has made a tube of dirt in which it will make its home.*

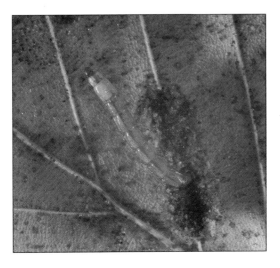

After heavy rain, pond water can become cloudy. This is because lots of tiny pieces of soil are washed into the pond. These pieces of dirt could harm animals and plants. They could clog up the **gills** of fish and the breathing tubes of insects.

If soil covers the leaves of plants, this makes it difficult for light to reach the leaves. Plants use the light from the sun to make food for themselves, so a soil covering makes it difficult for water plants to feed.

Tiny creatures can help to clear the water. They do this by 'glueing' little pieces of dirt together. These creatures are called bloodworms because they are blood-red in colour.

Bloodworms are not really worms. They are the **larvae** of a fly called a midge. They are caught for food by fish such as sticklebacks and trout. You can buy them as fish food from a shop.

You can watch how bloodworms clear dirty water. First, take some dead leaves and some soil and mix these with water. Put the mixture in a large jar. Notice how cloudy the water is. Then put your bloodworms in the water.

Watch the bloodworms for several days. They will start to make little tubes out of the dirt to live in. This cleans the water. Soon you will see that the water is very clear.

▶ *Bloodworms can be bought from aquarium shops.*

Water fleas

▲ *The water flea is very tiny. The black blobs are winter eggs that will hatch in the spring.*

In summer, many thousands of water fleas can appear in a pond. Although they are called water fleas, they are not like the type of fleas that bite. The best-known are called Daphnia.

Most water fleas are tiny and feed on microscopic green plants in the water. These plants are called **algae**. Algae get their energy from the sun and grow in parts of the pond where the light is the strongest. The water flea swims to the part of the pond where is can find the most algae in the water. You can find out how water fleas know where algae lie.

◄ *Damselfly nymphs catch and eat water fleas.*

Put some water fleas into a glass jar with some water. Allow them to settle for several hours. In the dark, shine a torch on to the side of the jar and watch what happens. If you like, you can use the darkened box that you made on page 11 and make a hole in the side to shine the torch. If the fleas move towards the light, you know they are looking for something to eat.

When water fleas eat algae, the energy that the algae have obtained from the sun gets passed on through the **food chain**. Plants such as algae are always at the beginning of the food chain. Water fleas in turn are eaten by **predators** such as damselfly nymphs. This is what such a food chain would look like:

▲ *You can watch your waterfleas through a darkened view-box.*

▼ *The food chain. Algae is eaten by water fleas. Water fleas are eaten by damselfly nymphs.*

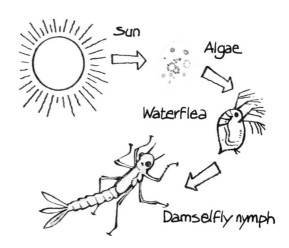

Sun

Algae

Waterflea

Damselfly nymph

Sticklebacks

Sticklebacks are small fish that are easy to catch in ponds and streams. You can keep sticklebacks in a tank but you must let them have some pondweed, and feed them every day.

▲ *The red throat of a male stickleback.*

▼ *A male stickleback builds a nest ready for its mate to lay eggs.*

In the spring, the throat of a male stickleback turns bright red to attract a **mate**. The male stickleback will also begin to build a nest for a female to lay her eggs. The stickleback has made this area his territory and he chases away other males that try to enter it. Rival males also have red throats in the spring.

When your male stickleback has started to build a nest you can study how he defends his territory.

Find out if the stickleback chases away his rivals by recognizing their shape, or by looking at their colour.

Using cardboard, cut out the shape of two sticklebacks and use felt-tip pens to colour one black and the other black with a red throat. Make a small circle and colour this red. Put each shape in to the water in turn. Each shape should be placed in the male's territory near his nest. Count how many times the stickleback attacks each shape.

What does this tell you about the male stickleback? Does he attack the fish-shape or does he just attack the colour red?

What happens if you now add another male stickleback to the tank?

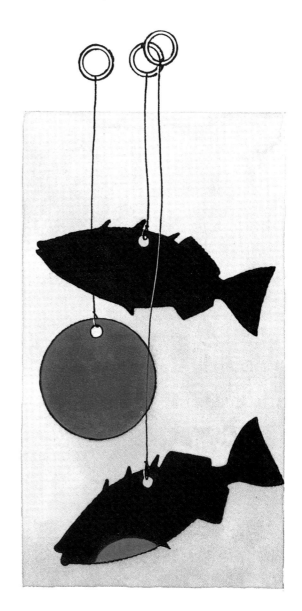

Make shapes like these to put in your tank.

Growing duckweed

Duckweed is often found floating on the surface of ponds. It is a very important food for fish. For duckweed to grow, it needs sunlight and water. You can find out if duckweed needs any other types of food called **nutrients**, to make it grow.

Nearly all of this pond has been covered by duckweed.

Half fill two glass dishes with **distilled water**. Now add a few drops of plant food to one of them and stir well. The plant food container has nutrients from the plant food.

The other container just with the distilled water has no nutrients at all.

Put twenty pieces of duckweed into each dish and put both dishes on the windowsill in the light.

After about four weeks, count the number of pieces of duckweed in the dishes. Are there more pieces of duckweed in the dish with the plant food? Do both lots of duckweed look green and healthy?

Ponds are often found near or on farmland. When it rains, some of the **fertilizer** the farmer puts on his fields is washed into the pond. This fertilizer increases the amount of nutrients in the pond. Do you think that this also helps plants like duckweed to grow?

▲ *A close-up picture of duckweed floating in water.*

▼ *You can see how well the duckweed has grown when it has been fed nutrients.*

With nutrients   Without nutrients

How hot or cold?

Comparing the temperature of pond water and air using thermometers.

Early in the morning the air can feel cold. By midday, the air has warmed up. By the evening when the sun goes down, it can feel cooler again. The air warms up and cools down during the day.

Do you think that frogs, dragonflies and water beetles find the water hot and cold during the day? Some of the animals like to hide in the mud when the sun becomes too hot, and fish may sink to the bottom where it is cooler.

You can find out if the water becomes very much warmer or cooler during the day by comparing it with how much the air changes in **temperature** during the day.

You will need to use two **thermometers** for this experiment. One takes the temperature of the water and the other takes the temperature of the air in the shade. Put the bulb of one thermometer in the water in a pond. An adult can do this by hanging the thermometer from a horizontal metal rod held by clamps. The other is also hung like this in the shade.

Take the temperature of both thermometers every hour during the day. When you have your results put them on a graph. Does the temperature of the water go up and down in the same way as the temperature of the air?

▶ *A diagram showing the range of temperature that can be found in the air and in the water during one day.*

▼ *Temperatures on a thermometer are measured in degrees Celsius. Can you read these temperatures?*

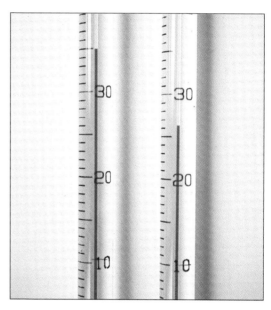

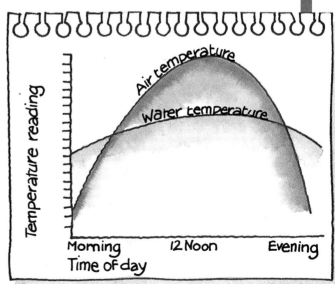

The water has a skin

▲ *The 'tail' of this scorpion is actually its breathing tube.*

There is a very thin skin on top of the water. Animals such as pond skaters use the surface. The pond-skater is a common bug that moves around the surface of the water without breaking the surface film or sinking in.

The skin is important in other ways too. It stops the breathing tubes of insects becoming flooded with water when they come to the surface to breathe. Some water spiders wait for insects to fall in the water and become trapped in the water skin. The spider then captures the insect. Pond-skaters feed like this too.

◄ *The pond-skater is resting on the water. Its little feet make tiny dents in the water skin.*

You can see how tough the skin of water is. Put a piece of tissue on top of some water in a dish. Gently lay a needle on the tissue. Soon the tissue will sink. Watch what happens to the skin of water when the needle rests on it. See what happens if you then add a drop of washing-up liquid to the water.

The skin of the water is damaged by pollution such as detergents. This means that the types of animals that use the skin of the water will die. Oil and washing-up liquids can destroy the surface. It is important that chemicals such as these are not allowed to pollute ponds and streams.

▲ *Can you see the dent the needle makes in the water film?*

▶ *Washing-up liquid has broken the water skin, so the needle falls to the bottom.*

Making a pond

▲ *These are the things you need to make a pond.*

You can easily make your own pond in your garden or school grounds. A small pond can be made from a washing up bowl. You will also need:

Large stones
Small logs
Flower pots
Soil and gravel
Pondweed

Dig a hole in the ground that is big enough for the bowl to sit in. Add some soil and gravel to the pond. Fill the pond with rain water. Buy some pond plants and put them in flower pots. The flower pots can be placed in the water around the edges of the pond.

◄ *The pond after it has been set up.*

A flat stone that just peeps out of the water will attract birds to bathe. It will also be a place where pond animals such as newts can crawl in and out of the pond.

You can wait for animals to come and live in the pond, but you would have to wait for several years for pond life to form naturally.

Instead of waiting for such a long time, you can add some plants such as duckweed, and mud from a natural pond. These will carry animals and their eggs. They will grow bigger in your pond. You will need to tend to your pond. Remove duckweed as it grows to stop it covering all of the pond.

▶ *This is the pond after five weeks.*

Key to ponds and streams

A key is a set of clues for naming living things. This will help you to identify some of the animals you will find in ponds and streams.

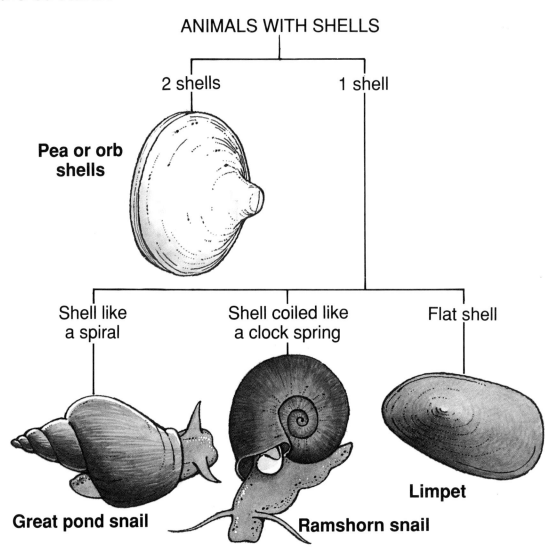

ANIMALS WITH SHELLS

2 shells   1 shell

Pea or orb shells

Shell like a spiral

Shell coiled like a clock spring

Flat shell

Great pond snail

Ramshorn snail

Limpet

ANIMALS WITHOUT SHELLS

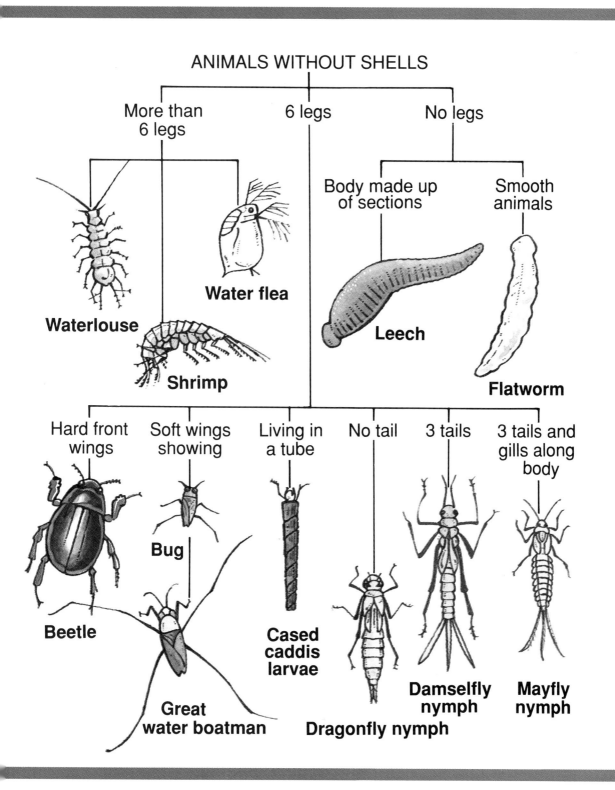

More than 6 legs

Waterlouse

Water flea

Shrimp

6 legs

No legs

Body made up of sections

Leech

Smooth animals

Flatworm

Hard front wings

Beetle

Soft wings showing

Bug

Great water boatman

Living in a tube

Cased caddis larvae

No tail

Dragonfly nymph

3 tails

Damselfly nymph

3 tails and gills along body

Mayfly nymph

GLOSSARY

Algae Simple plants. Some are microscopic, others large like seaweeds.

Bed The solid bottom of the stream.

Current The flow of water in the sea, river or stream.

Distilled water Water that has been turned into steam and then back into water.

Fertilizer A substance added to soil to make it richer.

Flow The movement of a liquid.

Food chain The feeding link between plants and animals.

Gills The organs that many water animals use to breathe.

Larvae The young of some animals including insects.

Nutrients Chemicals that plants need to grow.

Nymph The young of some insects.

Mate A breeding partner.

Oxygen A gas in the air that many animals need to stay alive.

Predators Animals that hunt and kill other animals for food.

Temperature The measure of how hot or cold something is, usually in $°$ C.

Thermometer A scientific instrument used for measuring temperature.

BOOKS TO READ

Aston, O. **Life in Ponds and Streams** (Macdonald, 1981)

Bown, D. **Pond** (Wayland, 1989)

Bown, D. **Stream** (Wayland, 1989)

Court, J. **Ponds and Streams** (Franklin Watts, 1985)

Milkins, C. **Discovering Ponds** (Wayland, 1989)

Swallow, S. **The Nature Trail Book of Ponds and Streams** (Usborne, 1980)

NOTES

p8-9 When studying ecology, sampling techniques need to be standardized when comparing one part of a pond or stream with another. When using a net to sweep the pond, it is important to have the same length of sweep in both the margins and the open water, otherwise it would not be a fair test.

p10-11 Usually, there are greater numbers of freshwater shrimps in flats than riffles. Leaves from the trees are the main food of shrimps, and they accumulate in the slower moving water of a flat. Leaves tend to be washed out of the riffles into the flats.

p12-13 The backswimmer will swim the 'right' way up if the light is shone from beneath.

p14-15 It is very important that the boiled water is allowed to cool to room temperature before the snails are put into it. For a fair test, the snails should be the same size. Different sized snails have different breathing frequencies regardless of oxygen availability.

p16-17 A good supply of bloodworms can be obtained from aquarium shops.

p18-19 The water flea is a crustacean. It can be purchased from aquarium shops. The water flea should gather on the side of the jar that has the light shining on it.

p20-21 The male stickleback is fiercely territorial. The common sense approach would lead us to think that the male attacks other males because he recognizes them and wants to defend his territory. This is not the case as the stickleback attacks the red circle more than the stickleback shape. Some males even ignore a male fish entering his territory to continue attacking the red circle.

p22-23 The water with the nutrients added will promote the most growth.

p24-25 Water remains at a very stable temperature. There will be a small increase in the water temperature during the day but not to the extent of the surrounding air.

p26-27 The needle is not floating in the water the way that a cork floats on water. It is being supported by the water skin or tension. This skin can be destroyed by oils and detergents and can lead to the death of wildlife.

INDEX

The pictures on page 18 were supplied by Oxford Scientific Films photographed by Chris Catton (top) and David Thompson (bottom).